D1232265

Benjamin Franklin's
Art of Virtue Journal

By Paula R. Benner

ISBN 0-7414-2980-2

Permission is hereby granted to copy the Personal Journal Chart, Franklin's Morning and Evening Questions, and the Certificate of Achievement for personal or educational uses.

Published by:

PUBLISHING.COM

1094 New DeHaven Street, Suite 100
West Conshohocken, PA 19428-2713
Info@buybooksontheweb.com
www.buybooksontheweb.com
Toll-free (877) BUY BOOK
Local Phone (610) 941-9999
Fax (610) 941-9959

Printed in the United States of America

Printed on Recycled Paper

Published June 2006

Ben's
Book
of
Virtues

Contents

Dedication

Happy 300th birthday, Benjamin Franklin! My gift, *Benjamin Franklin's Art of Virtue Journal*, is especially dedicated to children and youth, as well as their parents and teachers. May they overcome all obstacles[1] and secure the relationships, opportunities, skills, and values needed to succeed in life.

Acknowledgments

This book is offered as a tribute to the personal character and civic virtue of America's great sage, Benjamin Franklin. Let his wit and wisdom be impressed upon these pages. As he was unable to finish the "art of virtue," may this book help to fulfill his desire.

A special "thank you!" goes to Elizabeth Clare Prophet for first introducing me to Franklin's method through her lecture.[2] Mrs. Prophet's vast teachings of the saints and sages of East and West have helped me immeasurably in my pursuit of the "art of virtue."

Thanks to my teacher, Helen Collier, for her seminars on the scientific principles of success, as well as her encouragement and counsel.

I am grateful to the following authors for their works on Benjamin Franklin and his "art of virtue" (quoted herein, with their permission).

Paul Mountjoy wrote an article that I discovered that introduced me to Franklin's method of self-improvement. The interest and encouragement expressed by Professor Mountjoy during our telephone conversations were appreciated.

In their first issue of *Freedom Star News*, Marion and Carol Bogdanich expanded my awareness of the wellspring of Franklin's accomplishments. Included in their interesting article was reference to *Benjamin Franklin's The Art of Virtue* by George L. Rogers. This excellent book explains Franklin's formula for successful living and the 12 principles that guided his life.

Grateful acknowledgment is given to the Art Department of the Free Library of Philadelphia (Central Branch) for its excellent clip art collection. Most of the images used in this journal came from books produced by Dover Publications, Inc.

My heartfelt appreciation goes to my mother, Pat Soden, for her loving support and help in the household that gave me more time to devote to this project.

Two lab assistants at University of Pennsylvania computer laboratories were very helpful—James Robison and Brendon Burke. Staff at Penn's Information Systems and Computing—John Mulhern, III; Lee Gunter; and Michael Scherphorn— went the extra mile to assist me in resolving computer program problems.

The presence of Benjamin Franklin at his statues on the Penn campus was felt on the quiet summer nights spent typing this text.

I extend my gratitude to those who shared their time and talents in review of this journal. Wordsmiths Patricia Robertson and Sara Lee Langsam provided encouragement, moral and spiritual support, feedback, and food for thought on draft copies. Patricia Conant critiqued the graphics as well as the content. Margaret Holmes offered feedback on a draft version. When I thought I was finally finished, publishing coaches Nigel Yorwerth and Patricia Spadaro adeptly pointed out areas in the text that could benefit from revision.

Thank you, Joan Morrone and Robert Mongrande, for quickly responding to my call, your trust and kind helpfulness.

To those kindred souls who have been helpful during the writing of *Benjamin Franklin's Art of Virtue Journal*, thank you, one and all!

Enduring Achievements
of Benjamin Franklin

1706   Born on January 17 in Boston, Massachusetts

1729   Began publishing a successful newspaper, the *Pennsylvania Gazette*

1731   Founded the first public or circulating library

1732   Wrote and published the first edition of the acclaimed *Poor Richard's Almanack*

1736   Organized the first volunteer fire brigade in Philadelphia

1742   Wrote proposals resulting in the creation of an academy that became the University of Pennsylvania
       Invented the Franklin Stove

1743   Proposed that men of science and learning unite to form the American Philosophical Society

1747   Organized the first Militia

1752   Performed a dangerous electrical experiment, drawing lightning down from a storm cloud with a kite
       Founded the first fire insurance company in America

1753   Invented the lightning rod

1775   Drafted and presented to Congress his *Articles of Confederation and Perpetual Union,* the first plan to unite the North American colonies

1776   Served as a member of the drafting committee to submit the Declaration of Independence to Congress
Signed the Declaration of Independence
Presided at the Pennsylvania Constitutional Convention

1778   Convinced the French government to sign the Treaty of Alliance with the United States

1782   Helped negotiate the Treaty of Peace with Great Britain

1784   Negotiated treaties with Prussia and other European countries
Invented bifocals

1787   Was elected president of the Pennsylvania Society for Promoting the Abolition of Slavery
Served as delegate to the Constitutional Convention
Signed the United States Constitution

1789   Signed a petition to the first Congress of the United States calling for an end to slavery

1790   Died on April 17

2006   Ben's 300th birthday is celebrated across the nation throughout the year

PART ONE

Benjamin Franklin:
Renaissance Man

Preface

Who should read this book? It was designed for use by youth and adults alike. Parents, teachers, people who care about youth, and all who seek self-betterment can benefit from Benjamin Franklin's counsel.

Why should you read this book? Historian Arnold Toynbee described the chaos that marks the disintegration of civilization as a "time of troubles." We only need to look around us to see that we live in a world of crisis. Severe, unpredictable weather patterns have left a trail of devastation. Bob Sherman, the CEO and Executive Director of the Character Education Partnership, expounded upon a challenge besetting our youth.

> Investigations and the ensuing bombardment of media coverage have pulled back the curtain of American professional life and revealed a landscape that is painfully short on models of principled behavior. . .the Associated Press reported that 70% of people polled believe that kids today have worse manners than children of previous generations. Though disappointing, the decline in proper etiquette is not at all surprising when you consider the behavior of the role models that children are expected to emulate.[3]

Toynbee suggested surviving the chaos and preventing a collapse by a process of spiritualization from within. This "etherialization" is key to the success of the experiment in freedom for which America was founded. It is my hope that the practice of Benjamin Franklin's "art of virtue" will help reverse these alarming trends, thus contributing to the perpetuity of cherished American values and traditions.

The system of self-improvement that you are invited to experiment with in *Benjamin Franklin's Art of Virtue Journal* was first developed by Benjamin Franklin. His many achievements and strength of character are proof that his approach works. The words of Benjamin Franklin, with all their wit and wisdom, grace the pages throughout this book.

The variations in spelling and usage were found in Franklin's original text. His language was customary for the colonial period (of 18th century America) in which he lived. To help the reader navigate the excerpts from Franklin's autobiography, short summary statements precede quotations. Also, modern versions follow a select few of his proverbs.

This book consists of three parts. Part One provides background information on Franklin—his prolific life, quest for moral excellence and practical methods for achieving it. Instructions for using Parts and Three of the book are provided. The notes offer further details about some of the information presented.

In Part Two, the 13 virtues are presented in his sequence, along with corresponding illustrations and proverbs from Poor Richard. Franklin's proverbs have been rearranged to fit his 13 virtues.

My challenge was to write a modern version of the proverb that updated archaic language and made hidden meanings more explicit. The profundity of the proverbs made writing one sentence translations a difficult task. In this book, Franklin's proverbs are heralded by "then"; my revisions are marked by "now."

Part Three provides a number of forms that may be reproduced to facilitate the keeping of a personal journal using Franklin's approach. Franklin's virtue chart, his morning and evening questions, and space for drawing and story writing offer the reader opportunities for self-reflection.

Last but not least, be sure not to miss the Certificate of Achievement and the contest plan at the end of the book!

America's Renaissance Man

Throughout 2006, the nation commemorates the 300th anniversary of Benjamin Franklin's birth. The website of the Benjamin Franklin Tercentenary Commission acclaims Franklin as "one of the more extraordinary men of his time—and ours." He drew electricity from the heavens, shaped an independent and unified nation, and exemplified the American character. Franklin became famous as a civic leader, statesman, diplomat, founding father, revolutionary, the first Postmaster General of the U.S., scientist, inventor, printer, publisher, writer, philanthropist, and founder of educational institutions and the first lending library. Truly Franklin can be praised as a jack-of-all-trades—and a master of most of them.

The first issue of *Freedom Star News* (1994) gave tribute to the life of Benjamin Franklin.

> . . .He always put his knowledge into some practical project or invention. The Franklin stove, bifocals, the lightning rod and other experiments with electricity were some of these.
>
> He was constantly busy and seldom bored. In a letter to his mother in 1750, he stated that he would rather have it said "He lived usefully" than "He died rich." Franklin became intent on producing "something for the common benefit of mankind."

And produce he did! No matter how busy he was he always found time to try new ideas. He formed the first circulating library in America. He helped organize Philadelphia's fire department and a fire insurance company. He created a postal system to improve delivery time and became the first Postmaster General. He suggested ways to light the streets, dispose of garbage, and organized Pennsylvania's volunteer militia.

He worked with others to found one of America's first hospitals. In 1749 he proposed the creation of an academy and outlined the curriculum that he considered proper for such a school. In his typically practical fashion, he recommended emphasis on reading, writing and speaking the English language rather than various ancient languages taught in other schools. The purpose of this was to make the students into useful citizens, rather than learned scholars. This Philadelphia Academy grew to become the present University of Pennsylvania.

His name has been adopted by numerous American organizations. Franklin's ideas and inventions have become an integral part of American culture. John Adams praised him:

> His name was familiar to. . .such a degree that there was scarcely a. . .citizen. . .who was not familiar with it, and who did not consider him a friend to humankind. When they spoke of him, they seemed to think he was to restore the Golden Age.[4]

During the Renaissance period, men such as Michelangelo and Leonardo da Vinci became famous, not only as artists, but also as architects, engineers, inventors, and scientists. The attribution, Renaissance, has since been used to describe people who possess a genius, not only in one narrow specialization, but in broad areas of human knowledge. Franklin was invigorated by infinite interests and an exceptional range of accomplishments. He can truly be esteemed as America's first Renaissance man.

The Promise of Opportunity

In his book, *Benjamin Franklin*, author Chris Looby claims that Benjamin Franklin's most significant contribution was not any one of his achievements, great as they were, but rather, the way in which he lived. Virtually from nothing, Franklin forged a self-made path that led him to accomplishment and world renown. His life is a model of the American success story and the promise of opportunity bestowed upon every man, woman, and child.

Benjamin was born in 1706 in a Puritan family, the 15th of 17 children. They lived in a modest house in Boston. Three times each Sunday his poor but pious father, Josiah, led all his children to church. He taught them to be honest, hardworking, and satisfied with little.

Josiah trained Benjamin to work in his candle- and soap-making business, but he was discontented with this work. His father benevolently escorted Benjamin through the city streets to watch craftsmen at their jobs, hoping to find a trade that would interest the boy. Recognizing his son's intelligence and his love of learning, he sent him to apprentice in his older brother's print shop, where he would be surrounded by the printed word.

In the 1700's, books were uncommon—a luxury for the wealthy. Few children went to school, as it was also very costly. Although Benjamin only had two years of formal schooling, he developed a lifelong habit of independent study. Benjamin professed that he learned to read when he was very little. Books were his great passion.

As a young apprentice, Benjamin persuaded his employer to give his boarding money directly to him, as he could live on half of it and use the remainder for books. (The titles in his personal collection numbered over 4,000.) When he wasn't working, Benjamin was in his room reading every book he could find. He read insatiably on a multitude of subjects—at night, before work in the morning, and even on Sundays. He used the few hours he was able to steal from other activities for reading as well as writing.

Since Benjamin was no longer in school and had no teacher to help him, he decided to teach himself to write. He read portions of admired texts and rewrote them from memory. To determine the faults that needed correction, he compared his work with the original. To expand his vocabulary, Benjamin rewrote book chapters in the form of verse as well as sentences. His practice of taking notes on his reading on separate pieces of paper, shuffling them, and reassembling them in the proper sequence helped him order his writing and thinking. Through the repetition of these exercises, Benjamin's writing steadily progressed.

Fortunately, Benjamin had support in his earnest endeavors as well as his challenges. His father's frank feedback goaded Benjamin to improve his writing skills. When difficulties arose in his apprenticeship with James, his older brother, Benjamin often sought his father's advice.

At 17 years old, Benjamin had become a newspaper publisher, a good printer, and a celebrated author. As he could no longer tolerate James' harsh treatment, he decided to run away. After sneaking out of Boston, he faced a long and difficult journey, during which he trudged nearly three cold rainy days to his destination. Tired and dirty, with no money, no job, and no friends, Benjamin arrived in Philadelphia. Nevertheless, he felt positive that his fortune would finally improve. Indeed, the skills he worked so hard to develop would help him to become financially independent and successful in his vocations.

Poor Richard's Proverbs

In 1732, Benjamin Franklin launched his most successful business venture, *Poor Richard's Almanack*. Franklin's wit, wisdom, and humor made Poor Richard prosperous. This best seller in the colonies was widely read and highly regarded for a quarter of a century.

The sayings of Poor Richard did not all originate with Franklin. As this savant told us, these proverbs reflected "the wisdom of many ages and nations." However, Franklin often changed the words to make the maxims more pointed, meaningful, and understandable. His revisions have endured for centuries as part of our common speech.

The Key to Success

Through long hours of study and apprenticeship, Benjamin Franklin gained mastery in his undertakings. Step by step, he climbed the ladder of success. Was there a key to Franklin's great achievements—a key by which he drew lightning down from the heavens?

The energizing motive of Franklin's life was a burning desire to do good, to live usefully, and to help mankind. Whenever he saw a need, he sought to provide a solution. Yet, "Franklin's greatness lay not in either his talents or his achievements, as extraordinary as they were, but in his character" (Rogers, p. 11). As a boy, Benjamin was inspired by a book entitled *Essays to do Good* by Dr. Cotton Mather. Through the influence of this book, Franklin "always set a greater value on the character of a *doer of good* , than any other kind of reputation. . ." (Rogers, p. 12). In Franklin's view, his quest for moral perfection was the ultimate key to his success.

In approximately 1728, during his early manhood, Franklin conceived and executed a plan to improve his behavior. According to the research of Mountjoy and Sundberg (1981), Franklin's effort represented the first systematic approach to self-improvement. Thus, Franklin was also a pioneer in the field known today as behavioral science.

To communicate the principles of success to others, and especially to youth, was the main purpose of Benjamin Franklin's autobiography and his hope for the work he never finished, *The Art of Virtue*. His goal was to help youth understand what may be achieved through a consistent application of the principles of moral excellence, or virtue. In 1760, Franklin wrote on this subject to Lord Kames, a close friend.

I purpose. . .a little work for the benefit of youth, to be called *The Art of Virtue*. From the title I think you will hardly conjecture what the nature of the book may be. I must therefore explain it a little. Many people lead bad lives that would gladly live good ones, but do not know *how* to make the change. They have frequently *resolved* and *endeavored* it; but in vain, because their endeavors have not been properly conducted. To expect people to be good, to be just, to be temperate, &c., without *showing* them *how* they should *become* so, seems like the ineffectual charity mentioned by the Apostle, which consists in saying to the hungry, the cold, and the naked, "Be ye fed, be ye warmed, be ye clothed," without showing them how they should get food, fire, or clothing.

Most people have naturally *some* virtues, but none have naturally *all* the virtues. To *acquire* those that are wanting, and secure what we acquire, as well as those we have naturally, is as properly an art as painting, navigation, or architecture. If a man would become a painter, navigator, or architect, it is not enough that he is *advised* to be one, that he is *convinced* by the arguments of his adviser that it would be for his advantage to be one, and that he resolves to be one, but he must also be taught the principles of the art, be shown all the methods of working, and how to acquire the habits of using properly all the instruments; and thus regularly and gradually he arrives, by practice, at some perfection in the art. If he does not proceed thus, he is apt to meet with difficulties that discourage him, and make him drop the pursuit.

My *Art of Virtue* has also its instruments, and teaches the manner of using them. . ..Such as are naturally well disposed, and have been so carefully educated, as that good habits have been early established, and bad ones prevented, have less need for this art; but all may be more or less benefited by it. It is, in short, to be adapted for universal use (Bigelow, 3:257).

In his autobiography, Franklin described his method for self-improvement and explained why he was not able to complete *The Art of Virtue*:

. . .being fully persuaded of the utility and excellence of my method, and that it might be serviceable to people in all religions. . .I purposed writing a little comment on each virtue, in which I should have shown the advantages of possessing it, and the mischiefs attending its opposite vice; and I should have called my book *The Art of Virtue*. . . .

But it so happened that my intention of writing and publishing this comment was never fulfilled...the necessary close attention to private business in the earlier part of my life, and public business since, have occasioned my postponing it; for it, being connected in my mind with a *great and extensive project* that required the whole man to execute, and which an unforeseen succession of employs prevented my attending to, it has hitherto remained unfinished (Bigelow, 1:200-201).

Franklin's Method for Moral Perfection

The method Franklin used to cultivate a virtuous character is described below, in his own words.

It was about this time that I conceiv'd the bold and arduous project of arriving at moral perfection. I wish'd to live without committing any fault at any time; I would conquer all that either natural inclination, custom, or company might lead me into. As I knew, or thought I knew, what was right and wrong, I did not see why I might not always do the one and avoid the other. But I soon found I had undertaken a task of more difficulty than I had imagined. While my care was employ'd in guarding against one fault, I was often surprised by another; habit took the advantage of inattention; inclination was sometimes too strong for reason. I concluded, at length, that the mere speculative conviction that it was our interest to be completely virtuous, was not sufficient to prevent our slipping; and that the contrary habits must be broken, and good ones acquired and established, before we can have any dependance on a steady, uniform rectitude of conduct. For this purpose I therefore contrived the following method.

In the various enumerations of the moral virtues I had met with in my reading, I found the catalogue more or less numerous, as different writers included more or fewer ideas under the same name. Temperance, for example, was by some confined to eating and drinking, while by others it was extended to mean the moderating every other pleasure, appetite, inclination or passion, bodily or mental, even to our avarice and ambition. I propos'd to myself, for the sake of clearness, to use rather more names, with fewer ideas annex'd to each, than a few names with more ideas; and I included under thirteen names of virtues all that at that time occurr'd to me as necessary or desirable, and annexed to each a short precept, which fully express'd the extent I gave to its meaning (Bigelow, 1:188-189).

Franklin's thirteen virtues, with their principles for guiding behavior, are listed below:

Temperance   Eat not to dullness; drink not to elevation.

Silence   Speak not but what may benefit others or yourself: Avoid trifling conversation.

Order   Let all your things have their places; let each part of your business have its time.

Resolution   Resolve to perform what you ought; perform without fail what you resolve.

Frugality   Make no expense but to do good to others or yourself; i.e., waste nothing.

Indusry   Lose no time; be always employ'd in something useful; cut off all unnecessary actions.

Sincerity   Use no hurtful deceit; think innocently and justly; and, if you speak, speak accordingly.

Justice   Wrong none by doing injuries, or omitting the benefits that are your duty.

Moderation   Avoid extreams; forbear resenting injuries so much as you think they deserve.

Cleanliness   Tolerate no uncleanliness in body, cloaths, or habitation.

Tranquility   Be not disturbed at trifles, or at accidents common or unavoidable.

Chastity   Rarely use venery but for health or offspring, never to dulness, weakness, or the injury of your own or another's peace or reputation.

Humility   Imitate Jesus and Socrates (Bigelow, 1: 189-190).

To establish the habitual practice of these virtues, Franklin focused on one at a time, in a specific sequence.

My intention being to acquire the *habitude* of all these virtues, I judg'd it would be well not to distract my attention by attempting the whole at once, but to fix it on one of them at a time; and, when I should be master of that, then to proceed to another, and so on till I should have gone thro' the thirteen; and, as the previous acquisition of some might facilitate the acquisition of certain others, I arrang'd them with that view, as they stand above. Temperance first, as it tends to procure that coolness and clearness of head, which is so necessary where constant vigilance was to be kept up, and guard maintained against the unremitting attraction of ancient habits, and the force of perpetual temptations. This being acquir'd and establish'd, *Silence* would be more easy; and my desire being to gain knowledge at the same time that I improv'd in virtue, and considering that in conversation it was obtain'd rather by the use of the ears than of the tongue, and therefore wishing to break a habit I was getting into of prattling, punning and joking, which only made me acceptable to trifling company, I gave *Silence* the second place. This and the next, *Order*, I expected would allow me more time for attending to my project and my studies. *Resolution*, once become habitual, would keep me firm in my endeavours to obtain all the subsequent virtues; *Frugality* and Industry freeing me from my remaining debt, and producing affluence and independence, would make more easy the practice of Sincerity and Justice, etc., etc. Conceiving then, that, agreeable to the advice of Pythagoras in his *Golden Verses,*. . .daily examination would be necessary, I contrived the following method for conducting that examination.

He created a journal comprised of formatted pages for charting his behavior.

I made a little book, in which I allotted a page for each of the virtues. . . .I rul'd each page with red ink, so as to have seven columns, one for each day of the week, marking each column with a letter for the day. I cross'd these columns with thirteen red lines, marking the beginning of each line with the first letter of one of the virtues, on which line and in its proper column, I might mark, by a little black spot, every fault I found upon examination to have been committed respecting that virtue upon that day.

Form of the pages

TEMPERANCE						
Eat not to dullness; drink not to elevation.						
	S.	M.	T.	W.	T.	F.	S.

	S.	M.	T.	W.	T.	F.	S.
T.							
S.	*	*		*		*	
O.	**	*	*		*	*	*
R.			*			*	
F.		*			*		
I.			*				
S.							
J.							
M.							
C.							
T.							
C.							
H.							

Figure 1. Franklin's form for recording his own behavior.

When the first virtue was strengthened through a week's watch, he extended his attention to include the next as well. This cumulative approach allowed the completion of four courses (of the thirteen virtues) per year.

I determined to give a week's strict attention to each of the virtues successively. Thus, in the first week my great guard was to avoid every the least offence against *Temperance*, leaving the other virtues to their ordinary chance, only marking every evening the faults of the day. Thus, if in the first week I could keep my first line, marked T, clear of spots, I suppos'd the habit of that virtue so much strengthen'd, and its opposite weaken'd, that I might venture extending my attention to include the next, and for the following week keep both lines clear of spots. Proceeding thus to the last, I could go thro' a course compleat in thirteen weeks, and four courses in a year. And like him who, having a garden to weed, does not attempt to eradicate all the bad herbs at once, which would exceed his reach and his strength, but works on one of the beds at a time, and, having accomplish'd the first, proceeds to a second, so I should have, I hoped, the encouraging pleasure of seeing on my pages the progress I made in virtue, by clearing successively my lines of their spots, till in the end by a number of courses, I should be happy in viewing a clean book, after a thirteen weeks' daily examination.. . .(Bigelow, 1:188-195)

The precept of *Order* requiring that *every part of my business should have its allotted time,* one page in my little book contain'd the following scheme of employment for the twenty-four hours of a natural day.

Franklin's daily schedule is diagrammed on the following page.

THE MORNING. *Question.* What good shall I do this day?	5 6 7	Rise, wash and address Power- ful Goodness![5] Contrive day's business, and take the resolu- tion of the day; prosecute the present study, and breakfast.
	8 9 10 11	Work.
NOON.	12 1	Read, or overlook my accounts, and dine.
	2 3 4 5	Work.
EVENING. *Question.* What good have I done to-day?	6 7 8 9	Put things in their places. Sup- per. Music or diversion, or con- versation. Examination of the day.
NIGHT.	10 11 12 1 2 3 4	Sleep.

Figure 2. Franklin's "scheme of employment for the twenty-four hours of a natural day."

Following this plan for self-examination, Franklin's faults diminished.

I enter'd upon the execution of this plan for self-examination, and continu'd it with occasional intermissions for some time. I was surpris'd to find myself so much fuller of faults than I had imagined; but I had the satisfaction of seeing them diminish. To avoid the trouble of renewing now and then my little book, which, by scraping out the marks on the paper of old faults to make room for new ones in a new course, became full of holes, I transferr'd my tables and precepts to the ivory leaves of a memorandum book, in which the lines were drawn with red ink, that made a durable stain, and on those lines I mark'd my faults with a black-lead pencil, which marks I could easily wipe out with a wet sponge. After a while I went thro' one course only in a year, and afterward only one in several years, till at length I omitted them entirely, being employ'd in voyages and business abroad, with a multiplicity of affairs that interfered; but I always carried my little book with me.

The acquisition of order was most difficult for him.

My scheme of ORDER gave me the most trouble; and I found that, tho' it might be practicable where a man's business was such as to leave him the disposition of his time, that of a journeyman printer, for instance, it was not possible to be exactly observed by a master who must mix with the world and often receive people of business at their own hours. *Order*, too, with regard to places for things, papers, etc., I found extreamly difficult to acquire. I had not been early accustomed to it, and, having an exceeding good memory, I was not so sensible of the inconvenience attending want of method. This article, therefore, cost me so much painful attention and my faults in it vexed me so much, and I made so little progress in amendment, and had such frequent relapses that I was almost ready to give up the attempt, and content myself with a faulty character in that respect. . .for something, that pretended to be reason, was every now and then suggesting to me that such extream nicety as I exacted of myself might be a kind of foppery in morals, which, if it were known, would make me ridiculous; that a perfect character might be attended with the inconvenience of being envied and hated; and that a benevolent man should allow a few faults in himself, to keep his friends in countenance.

Although he never reached the perfection desired, Franklin believed that his striving made him a better and happier man.

In truth, I found myself incorrigible with respect to Order; and now I am grown old and my memory bad, I feel very sensibly the want of it. But, on the whole, tho' I never arrived at the perfection I had been so ambitious of obtaining, but fell far short of it, yet I was, by the endeavor, a better and happier man than I otherwise should have been if I had not attempted it; as those who aim at perfect writing by imitating the engraved copies, tho' they never reach the wish'd-for excellence of those copies, their hand is mended by the endeavour, and is tolerable while it continues fair and legible.

As his art of virtue brought Franklin happiness all his days, he hoped we would "follow the example and reap the benefit."

It may be well my posterity should be informed that to this little artifice, with the blessing of God, their ancestor ow'd the constant felicity of his life, down to his 79th year, in which this is written. What reverses may attend the remainder is in the hand of Providence; but, if they arrive, the reflection on past happiness enjoy'd ought to help his bearing them with more resignation. To Temperance he ascribes his long-continued health, and what is still left to him of a good constitution; to Industry and Frugality, the early easiness of his circumstances and acquisition of his fortune, with all that knowledge that enabled him to be an useful citizen, and obtained for him some degree of reputation among the learned; to Sincerity and Justice, the confidence of his country, and the honorable employs it conferred upon him; and to the joint influence of the whole mass of virtues, even in the imperfect state he was able to acquire them, all that evenness of temper, and that cheerfulness in conversation, which makes his company still sought for and agreeable even to his younger acquaintances. I hope, therefore, that some of my descendants may follow the example and reap the benefit.. . .(Bigelow, 1:196-200)

Heeding the advice of a friend, Franklin added a 13th virtue to his list—humility.

My list of virtues contain'd at first but twelve; but a Quaker friend having kindly informed me that I was generally thought proud; that my pride show'd itself frequently in conversation; that I was not content with being in the right when discussing any point, but was overbearing, and rather insolent, of which he convinc'd me by mentioning several instances; I determined endeavoring to cure myself, if I could, of this vice or folly among the rest, and I added *Humility* to my list, giving an extensive meaning to the word.

Franklin attributed his influence in public discourse to his successful efforts to alter his prideful speech.

I cannot boast of much success in acquiring the *reality* of this virtue, but I had a good deal with regard to the *appearance* of it. I made it a rule to forbear all direct contradiction to the sentiments of others, and all positive assertion of my own. I even forbid myself, agreeably to the old laws of our Junto, the use of every word or expression in the language that imported a fix'd opinion, such as *certainly, undoubtedly,* etc. and I adopted, instead of them, *I conceive, I apprehend,* or *I imagine* a thing to be so or so; or it *so appears to me at present.* When another asserted something that I thought an error, I deny'd myself the pleasure of contradicting him abruptly, and of showing immediately some absurdity in his proposition; and in answering I began by observing that in certain cases or circumstances his opinion would be right, but in the present case there *appear'd* or *seem'd* to me some difference, etc. I soon found the advantage of this change in my manner; the conversations I engag'd in went on more pleasantly. The modest way in which I propos'd my opinions procur'd them a readier reception and less contradiction; I had less mortification when I was found to be in the wrong, and I more easily prevail'd with others to give up their mistakes and join with me when I happened to be in the right.

And this mode, which I at first put on with some violence to natural inclination, became at length so easy, and so habitual to me, that perhaps for these fifty years past no one has ever heard a dogmatical expression escape me. And to this habit (after my character of integrity) I think it principally owing that I had early so much weight with my fellow-citizens when I proposed new institutions, or alterations in the old, and so much influence in public councils when I became a member; for I was but a bad speaker, never eloquent, subject to much hesitation in my choice of words, hardly correct in language, and yet I generally carried my points.

Even if he conceded to overcoming pride, Franklin admitted he would "probably be proud of my humility."

> In reality, there is, perhaps, no one of our natural passions so hard to subdue as *pride*. Disguise it, struggle with it, beat it down, stifle it, mortify it as much as one pleases, it is still alive, and will every now and then peep out and show itself; you will see it, perhaps, often in this history; for, even if I could conceive that I had compleatly overcome it, I should probably be proud of my humility (Bigelow, 1:201-203).

How to Use Parts Two and Three

Parts Two and Three of this book provide the reader with an opportunity to experiment with Franklin's methods. Below each virtue in Part Two is its precept assigned by Franklin. His precept is followed by an affirmation written by this author, along with space for the reader to make personal notes. The affirmations are written in simple language for young readers. However, the application may present a challenge, even for adults who would model the virtue for children.

Some parents may prefer not to present Franklin's chastity precept to children. Please note that the correlated affirmation makes no reference to sex. By replacing the precept with the affirmation, the chastity page may be comfortably used.

To get the best results from using *Benjamin Franklin's Art of Virtue Journal*, you are encouraged to respond, in writing, to Franklin's morning and evening questions. Journaling pages for this purpose are provided in Part Three. You may draw a picture or write a story about a virtue of your choice on the worksheet in this section.

In his book of charts, Franklin only noted his shortcomings; however, you may choose to note your victories on the Personal

Journal Chart. To help you track your progress with the virtues, the week number and dates can be entered in the blanks provided.

Students who successfully practice a virtue for a sustained period of time may be recognized with a Certificate of Achievement. An explanation for using this Certificate follows. In the corresponding blank, insert the name of the student and the school (or organization), the date of the award, and the virtue practiced by the student. To motivate student achievement, you may wish to hold them accountable to a specific period of time to qualify for recognition. The bottom line is reserved for official signatures (i.e., the principal and the teacher).

Above the date line on the certificate appears a reference to Benjamin Franklin's Society of the Free and Easy. On this topic, Karen Greene wrote the following:

> Lasting peace, Ben believed, can only be found in learning to practice virtue. He dreamed of an organization dedicated to using his plan. He named it The Society of the Free and Easy to show the tranquility that came to those who acquired virtue.

Perhaps you may qualify to be an honorary member. Together let us help Franklin launch this club.

Thank you for your interest in *Benjamin Franklin's Art of Virtue Journal.* It is my hope that this journal will be a helpful tool in your quest for self-improvement. Through our earnest application and the "law of Compensation"[6], we can make our world a better place.

> The body of B. Franklin, printer, like the cover of an old book, its contents torn out. . .lies here food for worms, but the work shall not be lost, for it will as he believed appear once more in a new and more elegant edition revised and corrected by the author.
>
> ∼ Benjamin Franklin[7]

Notes

1 See *Index of Leading Cultural Indicators 2001* at www.empower.org.

2 In her lecture "Ignorance of the Law Is No Excuse," Elizabeth Clare Prophet presented nine habits to cultivate in order to break the habit of ignorance. Her discussion included a review of Benjamin Franklin's unique system for self-improvement, which is the subject of this journal. For more information on Mrs. Prophet's work, please visit http://www.tsl.org, or call 1-800-245-5445.

3 Keynote address to Rotary Club of Dallas announcing Dallas Call to Character, October 19, 2005.

4 This quote is from a letter by John Adams to his wife, Abigail. See *John Adams* by David McCullough.

5 In his scheme of employment for the twenty-four hours of a natural day, Franklin refers to "Powerful Goodness." Religion was a powerful influence upon Franklin and an important part of his formula for living a successful life. On this subject, Franklin said the following:

> . . .I conclude that, believing a Providence, we have the foundation of all true religion; for we should love and revere the Deity for his goodness, and thank him for his benefits; we

should adore him for his wisdom, fear him for his power, and pray to him for his favor and protection. And this religion will be a powerful regulator of our actions, give us peace and tranquillity within our own minds, and render us benevolent, useful, and beneficial to others (Bigelow, 9:248).

The spiritual motivation directing Franklin's quest for virtue is expressed in his following statement taken from a prayer book that he made for his personal devotions.

I conceive for many Reasons that he is a good Being, and as I should be happy to have so wise, good, and powerful a Being my friend let me consider in what manner I shall make myself most acceptable to him.

Next to the Praise resulting from & due to his Wisdom, I believe he is pleas'd and delights in the Happiness of those he has created; and since without Virtue Man can have no Happiness in this World, I firmly believe he delights to see me Virtuous because he is pleas'd when he sees Me Happy (Bigelow, 1:321-322). [As a comment from this author on the variations in the case of the m/M of me, might Franklin be making a subtle reference to "the little me and the great me?" See *The Little Me and THE GREAT ME*, by Lou Austin (Capon Springs, West Virginia: The Partnership Foundation, 1957).]

To help him stay on course in his quest, Franklin included inspirational sayings in his journal. Among these were two verses from the Proverbs of Solomon (3:16-17) that speak of wisdom and virtue. Franklin elaborated upon this theme:

And conceiving God to be the fountain of wisdom, I thought it right and necessary to solicit his assistance for obtaining it;

to this end I formed the following little prayer, which was prefix'd to my tables of examination for daily use.

O powerful Goodness! bountiful Father! merciful Guide! Increase in me that wisdom which discovers my truest interest. Strengthen my resolutions to perform what that wisdom dictates. Accept any kind offices to thy other children as the only return in my power for thy continual favours to me (Bigelow, 1:195).

These passages by Franklin reveal his motives for striving to become virtuous. The practice of virtue makes him happy. Providence is pleased when he is happy. Franklin wants to become acceptable to the Deity so he can enter into friendship with Him. Accordingly, he prays every day for God's help and wisdom.

[6] In his essay, Emerson describes the principle of Compensation:

Every act rewards itself, or in other words integrates itself, in a twofold manner; first in the thing. . .and secondly in the circumstance.. . .Cause and effect, means and ends, seed and fruit, cannot be severed; for the effect already blooms in the cause, the end preexists in the means, the fruit in the seed.. . .Give and it shall be given you. (Emerson, R.W. "Compensation." *Essays: First Series.* 1841. Ralph Waldo Emerson Texts. May 2004. http://www.emersoncentral.com/compensation.htm.)

Did not Jesus Christ teach this same principle:

Whatsoever a man soweth, that shall he also reap (Galatians 6:7).. . .And let us not be weary in well doing: for in due season we shall reap if we faint not (Galatians 6:9).

How should one act in order to reap the rewards of a good harvest?

Is there one maxim which ought be acted upon throughout one's whole life? Surely it is the maxim of loving-kindness: Do not unto others what you would not have them do unto you.

~ Confucius

Eastern philosophy permits yet another perspective upon this principle.

Karma picks up where the golden rule leaves off. Do unto others as you would have them do unto you—*because someday it will be done unto you.* The Sanskrit word *karma* means "act," "action," "word" or "deed." The law of karma as it is traditionally taught says that our thoughts, words and deeds—positive and negative—create a chain of cause and effect, and that we will personally experience the effect of every cause we have set in motion. Karma, therefore, is our greatest benefactor, returning to us the good we have sent to others. It is also our greatest teacher, allowing us to learn from our mistakes. [Elizabeth Clare Prophet and Patricia R. Spadaro, *Karma and Reincarnation* (Corwin Springs, MT: Summit University Press, 2001), p. 9.]

Isaac Newton explained this principle in scientific terms in his third law of motion: For every action, there is an equal (in size) and opposite (in direction) reaction. You may have heard the saying, "What goes around, comes around." If Justice will (in due season) reward our efforts to increase Goodness, then is it not in our enlightened self-interest to do good?

[7] Ibid., p. 31.

[8] For a beautiful telling of "The Daffodil Principle" by Jaroldeen Asplund Edwards, visit http://llerrah.com/daffodilprinciple.htm.

[9] Elizabeth Clare Prophet and Patricia R. Spadaro, *Karma and Reincarnation.* Corwin Springs, MT: Summit University Press, 2001, p. 9.

[10] The song titled, "He Ain't Heavy, He's My Brother" was written by Robert William Scott and Sidney Keith Russell.

[11] The archaic word, venery, is defined as 1) indulgence in or pursuit of sexual activity, or 2) the act of sexual intercourse.

PART TWO

The Virtues Journal

Virtue #1

Temperance

Temperance

Then *Eat to live; live not to eat.*
Now *Eat for health and nourishment, not gluttonous delight.*

∾

Then *He that never eats too much, will never be lazy.*
Now *Eating the right amount energizes the body.*

∾

Then *'Tis easier to suppress the first Desire,*
than to satisfy all that follow it.
Now *Through self discipline, we gain freedom from*
enslavement to the appetities.

Temperance

Benjamin Franklin's precept: Eat not to dullness; drink not to elevation.

Affirmation: I make healthy choices about what I eat and drink.

Personal Reflections

_____
_____
_____
_____
_____
_____
_____
_____
_____
_____
_____
_____
_____
_____
_____
_____
_____
_____
_____
_____
_____
_____
_____

Virtue #2

Silence

Silence

Then *Teach your child to hold his tongue,*
he'll learn fast enough to speak.

Now *Teach your child to listen deeply from the heart, that no*
unkind words from his lips depart.

∾

Then *As we must account for every idle word,*
so we must for every idle silence.

Now *Cultivate the wisdom to know when to speak and when*
to be silent.

∾

Then *Half Wits talk much but say little.*

Now *Censure senseless chatter; save your energy for words that*
matter.

Silence

Benjamin Franklin's precept: Speak not but what may benefit others or yourself: avoid trifling conversation.
Affirmation: I speak when I have something helpful to say.

Personal Reflections

_____
_____
_____
_____
_____
_____
_____
_____
_____
_____
_____
_____
_____
_____
_____
_____
_____
_____
_____
_____
_____
_____
_____

Virtue #3

Order

Order

Then *Early to bed and early to rise, makes a man healthy, wealthy, and wise.*

Now *Keeping regular sleep times improves the sanity of the mind and the health of the body.*

∞

Then *Employ thy time well, if thou meanest to gain leisure.*

Now *Sow the labors of industry and reap the fruit of recreation.*

∞

Then *Have you somewhat to do to-morrow, do it today.*

Now *Don't procrastinate lest the opportunity be lost.*

Order

Benjamin Franklin's precept: Let all your things have their places; let each part of your business have its time.
Affirmation: I put everything where it belongs and make time for what is important.

Personal Reflections

_____
_____
_____
_____
_____
_____
_____
_____
_____
_____
_____
_____
_____
_____
_____
_____
_____
_____
_____
_____
_____
_____
_____
_____

Virtue #4

Resolution

Resolution

Then *Let no pleasure tempt thee, no profit allure thee, no ambition corrupt thee, no example sway thee, no persuasion move thee, to do any thing which thou knowest to be evil; so shalt thou always live jollily. . .*

Now *Steel the will to choose right lest the tempter steal your peace of mind.*

∾

Then *How few there are who have courage enough to own their own Faults, or resolution enough to mend them!*

Now *The exceptional individual combines the humble recognition of shortcomings with an unwavering effort to self-correct.*

∾

Then *Each year one vicious habit rooted out,
In time might make the worst Man good throughout.*

Now *The Daffodil Principle[8] reminds us to move lovingly toward our goals through daily effort, one step at a time.*

Resolution

Benjamin Franklin's precept: Resolve to perform what you ought; perform without fail what you resolve.
Affirmation: I faithfully do the things I should.

Personal Reflections

_____
_____
_____
_____
_____
_____
_____
_____
_____
_____
_____
_____
_____
_____
_____
_____
_____
_____
_____
_____
_____
_____
_____

Virtue #5

Frugality

Frugality

Then *For Age and Want save while you may;*
      No morning Sun lasts a whole Day.

Now *Save when you are able for scarcity or infirmity.*

∾

Then *A wise Man will desire no more, than what he may get*
      justly, use soberly, distribute chearfully, and leave
      contentedly.

Now *Want no more than that which you need, can use wisely,*
      give cheerfully, and surrender readily.

∾

Then *Who is rich? He that rejoices in his portion.*

Now *Gratitude for what you have is a sure path to prosperity.*

Frugality

Benjamin Franklin's precept: Make no expense but to do good to others or yourself; i.e., waste nothing.

Affirmation: I use my resources wisely to take care of myself and to help others.

Personal Reflections

_____
_____
_____
_____
_____
_____
_____
_____
_____
_____
_____
_____
_____
_____
_____
_____
_____
_____
_____
_____

Virtue #6

Industry

Industry

Then *Diligence is the mother of good luck.*
Now *Persistent right effort begets good fortune.*

∞

Then *Laziness travels so slowly that Poverty soon overtakes him.*
Now *To reap the harvest, one must sow and grow the seed.*

∞

Then *God helps them that help themselves.*
Now *Perseverance in well-directed effort attracts the creative forces of the universe to aid the endeavor.*

Industry

Benjamin Franklin's precept: Lose no time; be always employ'd in something useful; cut off all unnecessary actions.
Affirmation: I spend my time doing good, living usefully, and helping others.

Personal Reflections

_____
_____
_____
_____
_____
_____
_____
_____
_____
_____
_____
_____
_____
_____
_____
_____
_____
_____
_____
_____
_____
_____
_____
_____
_____

Virtue #7

Sincerity

Sincerity

Then *Hear no ill of a friend, nor speak any of an enemy.*
Now *To magnify the good, fix your vision on the tidbit of gold in the mud.*

∾

Then *What you would seem to be, be really.*
Now *Practice those virtues you desire to possess until the force of habit grants them irrevocably unto you.*

∾

Then *The same man cannot be both Friend and Flatterer.*
Now *Sincerity is the light of the soul, as pretense is its mask.*

Sincerity

Benjamin Franklin's precept: Use no hurtful deceit; think innocently and justly; and, if you speak, speak accordingly.
Affirmation: In my thoughts, feelings, words, and deeds, I want only the best for everyone.

Personal Reflections

_____
_____
_____
_____
_____
_____
_____
_____
_____
_____
_____
_____
_____
_____
_____
_____
_____
_____
_____
_____
_____
_____

Virtue #8

Justice

Justice

Then *Don't throw Stones at your Neighbours',*
       if your own Windows are Glass.
Now *"Do unto others as you would have them do unto*
       you–because someday it will be done unto you."⁹

∾

Then *It is better to take many injuries, than to give one.*
Now *The joy of living is in forgiving.*

∾

Then *If thou injurest Conscience, it will have its Revenge on*
       thee.
Now *Listen to the still, small Voice within the heart.*

Justice

Benjamin Franklin's precept: Wrong none by doing injuries, or omitting the benefits that are your duty.
Affirmation: I treat others the way I would like to be treated.

Personal Reflections

_____
_____
_____
_____
_____
_____
_____
_____
_____
_____
_____
_____
_____
_____
_____
_____
_____
_____
_____
_____

Virtue #9

Moderation

Moderation

Then   *He is a Governor that governs his Passions,*
          and he a Servant that serves them.
Now   *Moderate desires fit one to be content in any situation.*

∾

Then   *If Passion drives, Let Reason hold the Reins.*
Now   *Exercise self-restraint over inordinate desires.*

∾

Then   *In success, be moderate.*
Now   *Bridle ambition: gratefully celebrate your victories.*

Moderation

Benjamin Franklin's precept: Avoid extreams; forbear resenting injuries so much as you think they deserve.

Affirmation: I make balanced choices and practice patience with the shortcomings of others.

Personal Reflections

_____
_____
_____
_____
_____
_____
_____
_____
_____
_____
_____
_____
_____
_____
_____
_____
_____
_____
_____
_____
_____
_____

Virtue #10

Cleanliness

Cleanliness

Note: Poor Richard's proverbs did not address this topic.

Cleanliness

Benjamin Franklin's precept: Tolerate no uncleanliness in body, cloaths, or habitation.
Affirmation: I keep myself and my environment clean.

Personal Reflections

_____
_____
_____
_____
_____
_____
_____
_____
_____
_____
_____
_____
_____
_____
_____
_____
_____
_____
_____
_____
_____
_____

Virtue #11

Tranquility

Tranquility

Then   *Wink at small faults—remember thou hast great ones.*
Now   *Your actions will gather more of their kind before
returning to you for blessing or bane.*

∾

Then   *To bear other people's afflictions, every one has courage
and enough to spare.*
Now   *"He Ain't Heavy, He's My Brother."*[10]

∾

Then   *He that would live in peace & at ease,
Must not speak all he knows, nor judge all he sees.*
Now   *When you can forgive the little foibles of others, you will
find serenity.*

Tranquility

Benjamin Franklin's precept: Be not disturbed at trifles, or at accidents common or unavoidable.
Affirmation: I keep my peace and forgive others for their little slips.

Personal Reflections

_____
_____
_____
_____
_____
_____
_____
_____
_____
_____
_____
_____
_____
_____
_____
_____
_____
_____
_____
_____
_____
_____
_____
_____

Virtue #12

Chastity

Chastity

Then   *Seek Virtue, and, of that possest,*
        To Providence, resign the rest.
Now   *If you have virtue, everything else will follow.*

∾

Then   *Virtue and a Trade, are a Child's best Portion.*
Now   *Help your child develop good character and the*
        foundation for a successful livelihood.

∾

Then   *A good example is the best sermon.*
Now   *Lead by example, modeling those behaviors you desire*
        others to emulate.

Chastity

Benjamin Franklin's precept: Rarely use venery[11] but for health or offspring; never to dulness, weakness, or the injury of your own or another's peace or reputation.

Affirmation: I know the good, I love the good, and I do the good.

Personal Reflections

Virtue #13

Humility

Humility

Then   *The Proud hate Pride-in others.*

Now   *Those who hate pride mirrored in others are too blind to see it in themselves.*

༄

Then   *People who are wrapped up in themselves make small packages.*

Now   *Humility acknowledges the flow of Infinite Intelligence that expands the mind of man.*

༄

Then   *Humility makes great men twice honourable.*

Now   *Every day do your best; God will do the rest.*

Humility

Benjamin Franklin's precept: Imitate Jesus and Socrates.
Affirmation: I honor Goodness in all.

Personal Reflections

_____
_____
_____
_____
_____
_____
_____
_____
_____
_____
_____
_____
_____
_____
_____
_____
_____
_____
_____
_____

PART THREE

Your Personal Journal

Draw your own picture about a virtue.

Write a story about a virtue.

Personal Journal Chart

| Dates _____ | | | |
| Week No. _____ | | | |

VIRTUE	Sunday	Monday	Tuesday
Temperance			
Silence			
Order			
Resolution			
Frugality			
Industry			
Sincerity			
Justice			
Moderation			
Cleanliness			
Tranquility			
Chastity			
Humility			

Personal Journal Chart

| Dates | | | |

Wednesday	Thursday	Friday	Saturday

Benjamin Franklin's Morning Question:

"What good shall I do this day?"

_____
_____
_____
_____
_____
_____
_____
_____
_____
_____
_____
_____
_____
_____
_____
_____
_____
_____
_____
_____
_____
_____

Benjamin Franklin's Evening Questions:

"What good have I done today?"

_____

_____

_____

_____

_____

_____

_____

_____

_____

_____

_____

_____

_____

_____

_____

_____

_____

_____

_____

_____

_____

_____

_____

"Where have I strayed?"

_____
_____
_____
_____
_____
_____
_____
_____
_____
_____
_____
_____
_____

"What good have I omitted?"

_____
_____
_____
_____
_____
_____
_____
_____
_____
_____
_____
_____
_____

CERTIFICATE OF ACHIEVEMENT

This document certifies that

Student

School

has been awarded this certificate for successful practice of the virtue of

Date

and granted membership in Benjamin Franklin's Society of the Free and Easy

Principal

Teacher

References

Bigelow, John. *The Works of Benjamin Franklin*, 12 volumes. New York: G. P. Putman's Sons, 1904.

Franklin, Benjamin. *Poor Richard's Almanack*. Mount Vernon, New York: Peter Pauper Press, 1980.

Freedom Star News, Volume 1, No. 1. Turlock, CA: Fall 1994.

Greene, Karen. *Ben's Book of Virtues: Ben Franklin's Simple, Weekly Plan for Success and Happiness*. New Hope, PA: New Hope Press, 1994.

Looby, Christopher. *Benjamin Franklin*. Philadelphia, PA: Chelsea House Publishers, 1990.

Mountjoy, Paul T., and Sundberg, Mark L. "Ben Franklin the protobehaviorist I: Self-management of behavior." *The Psychological Record*, Vol. 31, No. 1 (Winter 1981), p. 13-24.

Rogers, George L. *Benjamin Franklin's The Art of Virtue. His Formula for Successful Living*. Midvale, UT: ChoiceSkills, Inc., 1996.

Benjamin Franklin's
Art of Virtue
Contest

To communicate the principles of success and self-improvement was Franklin's hope for the work he never finished, *The Art of Virtue*. Using his book of charts, he daily evaluated his progress in 13 virtues that he desired to master. Now you can learn how to use his method explained in the new release, *Benjamin Franklin's Art of Virtue Journal*. The contest outlined below is for readers of this book.

How have you, your family, friends, co-workers, or students (or those you know) benefitted from the use of *Benjamin Franklin's Art of Virtue Journal*? Which are your favorite parts of this book and why? What are your best responses to Benjamin Franklin's morning and evening questions? How has the journal helped you to overcome bad habits and to progress on the path of self-improvement? What is the value of the practice of the art of virtue? What do the proverbs of Poor Richard mean to you? How are they applicable today? We welcome your anecdotes about and interpretations of these timeless maxims.

Essay Topics Chose ONLY one of the following questions as per the guidelines listed above:

1. At the beginning and end of each day, Benjamin Franklin thought about doing good. How has the use of Benjamin Franklin's morning and evening questions helped you to plan and evaluate your own good works?

2. The proverbs of Poor Richard reflect "the wisdom of many ages and nations." Choose one and explain its meaning, with examples.

3. Benjamin Franklin believed that his quest for moral perfection was the ultimate key to his success. How has the use of this journal helped you to overcome bad habits and to progress on the path of self-improvement?

We await your response with joyous anticipation!